This book is dedicated to every
Australian wine consumer
and to the well-being
of their collections

WINE PRESS

Brisbane, Australia
www.cellaringwine.com
author@cellaringwine.com

First published in Australia by Wine Press 2002

National Library of Australia Cataloguing-in-Publication data:

Stelzer, Tyson, 1975- .
Cellaring wine: do-it-yourself solutions.
Includes index.
ISBN 0 9580628 0 3.
1. Wine - Storage - Australia. 2. Wine cellars - Australia.
I. Title.
641.220994

Photography, artwork and design by Tyson Stelzer
Typesetting by Wine Press
Printed by Openbook Print, Adelaide

Copyright © Tyson Stelzer 2002

No part of this book may be reproduced electronically, verbally or in print without written permission from the publisher, except in the case of brief quotations embodied in critical articles and reviews. The ideas presented may be freely replicated, adapted and further developed using refrigerators, polystyrene, timber and bottles of wine.

Caution:

Modification of any electrical appliance requires verification by a certified electrician. All 240V electrical work referred to in this book should be attempted only by a qualified person. To avoid risk of fire, timber, insulation and other such combustibles should be kept well away from refrigeration compressors, evaporators and electrical wiring. While the utmost care has been taken to ensure that the procedures outlined in this book are sound, the author accepts no responsibility for any consequences resulting from their interpretation. To ensure that projects are completed safely, readers should adhere to commonsense principles, always maintaining a healthy respect for power tools and electrical equipment.

Feedback:

Readers are invited to share their cellaring experiences and feedback with the author by emailing author@cellaringwine.com.

Cellaring Wine
do-it-yourself solutions

Tyson Stelzer

WINE PRESS

The Author

Tyson Stelzer is a dedicated wine enthusiast and freelance writer. His pursuits have led him to the depths of some of the world's greatest cellars. He has been lost in vineyards in France, stained his clothes working vintage in the Barossa and is regularly seen taking copious notes at every wine tasting he can get to. He also enjoys photography, physics, mathematics and building and restoring furniture. This book is a culmination of all of these passions. When he is not tinkering with his various cellars or visiting wine regions, he is teaching high school students or playing guitar and sax in his church's band. Tyson lives in Brisbane with his wife Rachael. He maintains that good wine deserves to be shared with good friends, and is best enjoyed in sensible quantities.

Contents

Introduction	1
1. The Rewards of the Cellar Why cellar wine?	3
2. The Secrets of All Great Cellars Six steps to creating perfect conditions	7
3. Near Enough? Assessing your storage locations	17
4. Where do I Start? A beginner's cellar	21
5. Raid the Fridge A climate-controlled cellar for $120	25
6. When Size Does Matter A cellar for 250 bottles	31
7. Visions of Grandeur A custom cellar cabinet	41
8. Moisture Matters Controlling humidity in the cellar	53
Index	57

Cellaring Wine: do-it-yourself solutions

Introduction

Ninety percent of wine is consumed within three hours of leaving the bottle shop. Perhaps once correct, this commonly quoted statistic is not quite so true today. The drinking habits of Australians are maturing, as we learn that our wines will do the same. Increasingly, we are appreciating the merits of aged wines.

There have always been the privileged few who maintain state-of-the-art cellars, safeguarding hundreds or even thousands of bottles. But more and more the average consumer is putting bottles aside to be blessed by the rewards of bottle age: a couple of cases stashed in the linen cupboard, a few dozen in the wine rack, a hundred bottles tucked away under the house. There are few greater joys than sharing a carefully cellared old bottle with good friends. And there are few greater disappointments than finding that the prized bottle has been spoilt by careless treatment. Many well-meaning 'hobby collectors' are oblivious to the reality that their storage conditions are slowly but surely killing their wines.

A number of years ago I set about establishing a small cellar of wines in my rented home in Brisbane, Queensland. I was told that this was an impossible task in our harsh subtropical climate, unless I was prepared to spend a small fortune. With a little creativity and perseverance, I have discovered otherwise.

My pursuit of information on budget cellaring has been a far-reaching endeavour. When it became apparent that there was nothing in print, I turned my questions to winemakers, wine consumers and wine experts across Australia and across the world. Where the answers were not clear, I returned to my scientific training and devised experiments that would provide the answers. This book is the culmination of these endeavours. It sets out to unravel the secrets of cost-effective home cellaring.

Numerous books have been written on how to build large and expensive cellars and on choosing wines to stock them. This book does not attempt to address either of these topics. Rather, it is dedicated to the hobby collector, and to the well-being of his or her humble but nonetheless prized wine collection.

Cellaring Wine: do-it-yourself solutions

1. The Rewards of the Cellar

Why cellar wine?

Purchasing wine is very much like purchasing a new plant for the garden. It is not often that I do either purely for what they represent at the time of purchase. But, with a little care and nurture, both can blossom into something much greater.

Wine is capable of amazing, indeed miraculous, transformations in the cellar. My fascination with this began with a humble case of 1995 Orlando Jacob's Creek Shiraz Cabernet. This was quite an investment for a student, and the case gained pride of place in the bottom corner of my linen cupboard. I finished the last two bottles of that case three years later, and they were the best bottles of the lot. Although I only paid $6.50 per bottle for this humble commercial wine from an average vintage, I was impressed by the way that it had integrated and developed after just a few years in relatively poor storage.

At the other end of the spectrum, I had the opportunity to taste a bottle of Penfolds Grange from the same vintage as the Jacob's Creek when it was released a couple of years ago. It was far too young to be drunk at the time, and I was left wondering just why there was so much hype surrounding this icon wine.

The answer came a year later at a dinner party with some good friends. Our host served a red wine, blind (masked), as is our tradition. It was big and dark, with only slight bricking in the colour. The nose was quite complex, meaty at first, but quite closed. As the wine opened up, it developed hints of tobacco, cedar, coffee, liquorice, chocolate and echoes of berry fruit. The palate was in perfect harmony with the nose. Everything was there — huge intensity, rich aged complexity but still hints of its origins, pronounced tannins and acid but in perfect balance with everything else. Oak was beautifully integrated, and the length lasted many minutes. When guessing time came around, I made a stab at early '90s. Hence my surprise when the wine was revealed to be a 1976. At 25 years of age, this old Grange really shone, and it still had the potential for many years ahead of it.

Some of us may tire of the simplicity of wines like Jacob's Creek, while

Cellaring Wine: do-it-yourself solutions

Grange is, and will forever be, out of reach for most of us. But between these two extremes lie a plethora of wines of exceptional quality and value. In Australia, we are privileged to celebrate the widest variety and highest calibre of value-for-money wines in the world. But in order to ensure that they drink at their best, a significant number of these require some bottle age.

Wines grow up in much the same way as we do. With enough patience, they mature to lose their rough edges, no longer grating on our senses. A multi-faceted personality emerges, replacing the simplicity of its younger self with a far deeper interest. It becomes much more pleasant and appropriate company at the dinner table, complementing rather than dominating. White wines like Rieslings and Semillons relinquish their racy acidity to take on a gloriously rich complexity of toast, honey and dried fruits. In reds, tannins soften as vibrant fruit freshness gives way to a more mature temperament of smooth fruit and secondary characters resembling flavours like chocolate, tobacco and mushroom. Exactly where in this progression it is at the prime of its life depends entirely on your taste.

The potential for saving money is a further bonus in cellaring wine. Penfolds Bin 28 Kalimna Shiraz is one of my favorite value-for-money commercial wines. When the excellent 1996 vintage was first released, I stocked up at just under $14 per bottle. As I write, the 1999 is current, and any price less than $18 is a bargain. The rare bottle shop that still stocks the 1996 is likely to charge $30–$40. A well-stocked cellar affords the luxury of always drinking the best vintages, and often at bargain prices.

You would hardly bring a plant home from the nursery, cut off the flowers, arrange them in a vase and throw away the rest of the plant. In the same way, patience with particular wines will be rewarded. Before we can reap this reward, we first need to know how to care for the 'plant'.

The Rewards of the Cellar

A vertical tasting at Pichon Longueville de Baron. Such great wines of Bordeaux do not just deserve extended cellaring: they positively demand it.

Cellaring Wine: do-it-yourself solutions

The private cellars of Château Margaux, Bordeaux

Cellaring Wine

The 6 conditions common to all great cellars

- Stable Temperature.
- Low Temperature.
- Adequate Humidity.
- Darkness.
- No Vibration.

Indexing your wines is vital.

- Use a manual system or a computer program. *
- Apply Vinoté Tags so every bottle is traceable. **
- Record every bottle going in and out.
- Keep track of the best time to drink each bottle.

* www.vinote.com/cellarsoftware.php — a comprehensive list of the world's best wine cellar programs.

** **Vinoté tag**
- Indestructible
- Everlasting
- Individually numbered
- Easily read

Cellar with Confidence

www.vinote.com

Vinoté Limited, P.O. Box 6564, Palmerston North, NZ. Ph. + 64 6 3549126

Vinoté products Manual Wine Catalogues, Cellar Management software, Vinoté Neck Tags, Barcode Scanners, **Cellar Thermometers**, Breatheasys, Label Lifters, Wine Pods, and other wine accessories.
NZ Distributors of Cellaring Wine do-it-yourself solutions.

2. The Secrets of All Great Cellars

Six steps to perfect conditions

When I bring a plant home from the nursery, I check the tag for the conditions that the plant appreciates, and accordingly choose the best location in the garden. I would not expect it to survive if I left it in the harshest corner of my yard and neglected to water and fertilise it.

Regrettably, this is just what some people do with their wines. The wine rack in the dining room and the cupboard above the refrigerator are not friendly environments for cellaring wines. A friend recently showed me a very attractive wine rack that he had built in his new kitchen. The only problem was that, after only a few weeks, many of his wines were showing signs of leaking around the corks. It is important to distinguish at this point between 'cellaring' and merely 'storing' wines. If they are stored for consumption within a number of months, such locations are probably quite satisfactory. But if wines are cellared for the purpose of developing maturity, then the right conditions are very important. Wine is in many ways a living and breathing thing and will respond to the conditions in which it is placed.

Sharing great old wines with like-minded wine enthusiasts must rank among life's most enjoyable experiences. I meet with a group of such friends for theme tastings throughout the year. We recently had the privilege of sharing a bottle of the rare 1969 Lake's Folly Hunter Valley Estate Dry Red. It was provided by one of our number as a mystery wine to supplement a vertical tasting of 1992–1998 Lake's Folly Cabernets, the more recent version of the same wine. The 1969 was quite superb, displaying layers of complexity and intensity of which its younger siblings showed mere reflections. It was a smooth but intense wine, perfectly integrated and balanced, simultaneously exuding hints of sweet fruit, chocolate, honey, coffee, leather and smoke, as well as some gamey and medicinal characters. Before it was unveiled, the group decided that it must be no more than a decade older than our 1990s line up. The extraordinary quality of this wine after more than three decades must, in part, be attributed to the cellaring conditions that it enjoyed in Lake's Folly's cellar during this time.

Cellaring Wine: do-it-yourself solutions

These conditions are common to all great cellars. Let's take a look at exactly what they are.

1. Stable temperature

A constant temperature is the single most important prerequisite for cellaring wines long-term.

Consider an unfortunate bottle of wine in my friend's kitchen wine rack. On an average day the wine might be stable at, say, 24°C, but in summer, the room may heat up to 30°C. At the same time, the wine in the bottle is likely to warm up to at least 27°C. In doing so, the liquid naturally expands, possibly even pushing the cork out slightly or causing a small amount of wine to be expelled around the cork. (This will quickly evaporate but may leave a slight residue under the capsule.) This movement has also weakened the seal of the cork. When the temperature drops again, the wine cools, contracts and may consequently draw a small amount of air into the bottle around the cork. It is here that the biggest problem lies. This can occur even if the wine does not leak past the cork. (Leakage can easily be identified by stiff capsules that resist rotation.)

Throughout the bottling procedure, the winemaker works hard to very carefully limit any contact the wine has with oxygen. Excessive contact results in oxidation, a chemical reaction that causes the wine to age prematurely, ultimately making it flat and lifeless. Colour deteriorates, aroma and fruit flavour diminish quickly and the wine may become bitter. Such avoidance of oxidation is even more important during the cellaring process. If oxygen is allowed to pass into the bottle around the cork, the quality of the wine will slowly deteriorate.

While stable temperature is the most important factor in cellaring wine, it can also be one of the most difficult to achieve. Australia is hardly renowned for its mild climate and gentle temperature variations! Cellaring of wine in most parts of our country therefore requires the deliberate provision of a stable temperature. At my home in Brisbane, the annual room temperature varies from around 9 °C to 38°C. A bottle of wine stored under such conditions will fluctuate from about 14°C to 32 °C. Even a 10°C annual variation, as is common in many Australian cellars, is said to be too large for reliable long-term cellaring.

More of a problem, however, is that of rapid temperature change. Seasonal variations aside, the daily temperature variation in our house is often in the order of 10°C. This results in a fluctuation of some 2–3°C in the temperature of wine in the bottle during an average day. Such conditions will cause a wine to deteriorate rapidly.

So what is ideal? The smaller the variation, the better. Although it is difficult to pinpoint exact numerical standards, I propose that excellent results would be achieved if one could maintain a daily bottle temperature variation of less than 0.5°C, a weekly variation of less than 1°C, and a yearly variation of not more than 5°C.

Hugel is a one of the most significant wine producers in the Alsace region of north-eastern France. Under its Riquewihr premises, it cellars its Rieslings and Gewurztraminers for up to ten years before releasing them. The temperatures in this cellar vary annually from around 12°C to 14°C. Such fluctuation is quite satisfactory, even for these very delicate varietals.

2. Low temperature

It is a common misconception that low temperature is the most important characteristic of a good cellar. It is not. It must take second place to a stable temperature. Nonetheless, it is an important second place.

The chemical reactions that occur in a wine as it ages are incredibly complex, and in fact not fully understood. However, as with most chemical reactions, their rate is dependent upon the ambient (surrounding) temperature. At

Fourth century chalk mines, now Champagne cellars at Tattinger, Reims. At 12m below the surface the temperature plummets to 10°C, at 18m it drops to 8°C.

high temperatures, say 25°C, these reactions will progress at such a rate as to develop the wine very quickly, effectively 'cooking' it. At low temperatures, below 10°C, the wine will develop very slowly indeed, virtually freezing into immobility. Somewhere between these extremes lies an ideal compromise, a temperature at which the wine ages slowly and elegantly, but still quickly enough that it does not need to be set aside for one's grandchildren. This temperature is commonly accepted to be 15°C. In reality, any constant temperature between about 12°C and 17°C is satisfactory.

White wines tend to prefer a slightly lower temperature and sparkling wines even more so. In the ancient old chalk caverns under Champagne, temperatures are usually between 10°C and 14°C. As one descends to eighteen metres below the surface, the thermometer drops to 8°C. Here the greatest of all sparkling wines mature very slowly indeed.

3. Adequate humidity

Fussy little creatures, these wines! Once we have achieved a stable temperature of 15°C, the next thing to look at is the relative humidity. In order to understand this we need to consider how the wine is sealed.

The 'inner sanctum' of Marc Bredif's tenth century rock cellars in the Loire Valley, France. Here, 13°C and 90% humidity sustain 128-year-old bottles.

The Secrets of All Great Cellars

Wine bottles are traditionally closed with the humble old cork, and although we are now seeing a number of better alternatives, alas, corks will still be with us for a long time to come. Being a natural substance, corks are somewhat prone to deterioration. They will not remain effective for long unless they are looked after. The easiest way to kill a cork is to dry it out. It will then shrivel, lose its seal, and the wine may begin to leak out of the bottle.

The cork can easily be kept moist on the inside by laying the bottle on its side to maintain contact between the cork and the wine. Keeping the outside from drying out requires a little more attention, and is best achieved by maintaining adequate humidity. Relative humidity around 70–80% is considered ideal. If the humidity is consistently below 60%, the cork will dry out.

Humidity throughout the ancient cellars of the old-world wine regions is regularly in the 80–100% range. At Marc Bredif in the Loire Valley in France, the innermost room of the cellar maintains a dead stable temperature of 13°C and a humidity of 90%. Vintages all the way back to 1874 lie perfectly preserved to this day. Well, almost perfectly. (I told you these bottles were fussy!) Bredif has recently constructed a very sterile climate-controlled warehouse to protect its new wines from excess moisture. Humidity above about 85% can cause labels to peel, cartons to rot and bottles to develop mould.

Château de Pommard has a different approach in its Burgundy cellars. At 14°C and very high humidity, the mould is apparent even on one-year-old bottles. By the time they are ready for release at ten years of age, a thick jacket makes it difficult to even distinguish one bottle from the next. But this is of little

Mould growing on a gate within the cellars of Château de Pommard

11

concern, as they are quickly washed, labelled and dispatched, looking just like new — and, incidentally, also tasting just like new. At twelve years of age, the 1989 Château de Pommard was a vibrant red-purple with hardly any browning in the colour whatsoever. The fresh raspberry fruit of the palate was more reminiscent of a two-year-old wine than a twelve-year-old. Ideal conditions can facilitate exceptional longevity.

At home we are not so fortunate as to be able to relabel every mouldy bottle. If you want that prized wine that you've been cellaring for years to look its best when it finally reaches the dinner table, keep it below 80% humidity. Otherwise the label may emerge at best unattractive, and at worst, unreadable.

4. Darkness

The very best underground cellars are cold, incredibly stable, moist and dank, and of course, very dark. Wines are creatures of the night, emerging from their long hibernation for just one moment of glory. But that moment will be less than glorious if the wine has spent its hibernation continually on display.

It has been verified that exposure to light produces chemical reactions in wine that cause it to deteriorate. In particular, ultraviolet light has the greatest effect, and white wines and champagnes are the most vulnerable. Amber-coloured bottles provide very good protection, but regrettably these have long ago fallen out of fashion to their much less protective clear and green counterparts. Consequently, the best solution is to keep the cellar in complete darkness whenever it is unattended. Intermittent artificial light will have minimal effect, but daylight should be avoided.

5. No vibration

If you are able to satisfy the demands of the first four conditions for cellaring wines, you are doing very well indeed. The last two are of lower consequence, but are worth considering for the best results. The first of these is the avoidance of disruption to the wines, both in the form of movement of the bottles and of vibration.

The Secrets of All Great Cellars

Guigal's impressive new cellar under Ampuis is fully temperature controlled, and insulated from the vibration of the main road above

Guigal is the most important producer in the famous Côte-Rôtie region of France's Rhone Valley. Outgrowing its 300-year-old cellars in Ampuis, it recently embarked on an enormous construction project. The result is almost two hectares of cellar caverns, climate controlled to 13°C and 80% relative humidity. This proved to be something of an engineering nightmare, with the facility sandwiched between the mighty Rhone river and a train line on one side, and a main road on the other. The finished product not only supports the road, but also Guigal's production facility, with a mass of some five tonnes per square metre!

Traffic rumbling across the top of the cellar is detrimental to the wine. Understanding this requires a little insight into the way in which wine develops. Put simply, the chemical processes in the wine produce larger and more complex molecules that eventually fall out of the solution as sediment. Under stable conditions, these are able to settle along the bottom of the bottle or barrel, allowing the wine to develop fully. Movement disrupts this process, stirring the sediment and mixing it throughout the wine.

The solution at Guigal was to construct an advanced anti-vibration system throughout the entire cellar structure. While most of us do not have the problem of trucks rumbling over our wine collection at home, vibration can still pose a threat. Mechanical cooling units are prime culprits.

Further to this problem, there are extreme phenomena such as 'travel shock', which the wine can experience after extended transportation. It may take weeks or even months to settle before it is again at its best. Closely related is 'bottle shock', where the wine takes some time to recover from the bottling process.

6. Low ventilation

Ventilation can be damaging to wines because it can upset the delicate temperature balance in the cellar. While gentle air currents in themselves are of little consequence, the danger arises when these currents vary the temperature in all or part of the cellar. In particular, artificial cooling units have a tendency to introduce cold air currents.

There needs to be a compromise here. On the one hand, moving air can be a necessity in maintaining a stable temperature throughout the cellar. In doing so, however, the air should not be of such a temperature, or moved so quickly, as to cause rapid fluctuations in bottle temperature. This naturally presupposes that the temperature can vary in different parts of the cellar, and this in itself should be avoided if possible. Where absolute perfection cannot be attained, it is sufficient to ensure that stiff breezes directed at the bottles are avoided, particularly if they have the potential to change the bottle temperature.

The Secrets of All Great Cellars

There will always be sceptics who challenge the significance of a good cellar. The evidence presented will be anecdotal and subjective. Invariably, a particular old bottle will be cited, having been stored under imperfect conditions, consumed at a ripe old age, and praised wholeheartedly. My response is simple: These critics may never know just how much better that bottle could have been.

It was a Barossa winemaker who first suggested to me that the best investment a wine collector can ever make is to establish ideal conditions in his or her cellar. At first impression it may appear that this is an impossible task for the hobby wine collector with a small collection and an even smaller budget. For those who are better endowed financially, there are numerous options available:

- Underground cellar (~$10 000)
- Aboveground cellar with a commercial cooling unit (~$8000)
- Commercial wine storage cabinet ($3000–$8000)
- Commercial control unit attached to a domestic refrigerator (>$500)
- Polystyrene wine boxes (~$60 per dozen bottles)
- Professional wine storage (~$700 for 100 bottles over five years)

I have many friends who successfully make use of such solutions, and I thoroughly recommend them for those who can afford them. But for those of us who cannot justify this expense, there has in the past been little alternative but to put up with grossly imperfect storage conditions. This is no longer the case. Across Australia, wine consumers are beginning to utilise cellaring solutions that are not only practical and ingeniously simple, but are at the same time as effective, and in some cases more effective, than many commercial alternatives. The following chapters detail four such solutions that have been successful for me.

Cellaring Wine: do-it-yourself solutions

A digital thermometer can easily be converted into a device for measuring bottle temperature in the cellar

3. Near Enough?

Assessing your storage locations

I have a friend who has a cellar under his house on the Gold Coast. The house is on a steep hill, with the cellar cut into the hillside such that most of it lies underground. The walls are Besser brick and the exposed side is well protected from the elements by a dense garden. He described it to me as the perfect cellar: moist, cool in summer and warm in winter. But ultimately the thermometer was the true judge. With a winter minimum of 13°C and a summer maximum of 27°C, the wine in his bottles was experiencing at least 10°C of annual variation. The first rule of assessing cellar suitability is that subjective judgements can be misleading.

My cellar holds its temperature to within a degree of 15°C. When I open it in summer I am confronted by a mass of cold air. It feels like a refrigerator. When I opened it last winter I got an unpleasant shock. It was warm in there! After a mild panic, I checked the thermometer and was relieved to find that it was still at exactly 15°C. Good pilots rely not on their perceptions but on their instruments. There's a lesson in that.

Cellar monitoring instruments

The most important instrument for monitoring a cellar is a thermometer with the capacity to record maximum and minimum temperatures. Two types are available: the traditional double-bulb thermometer, and more recently, the digital thermometer. I picked up an 'Acme' version of the latter at Woolworths a couple of years ago (Wile E. Coyote would be impressed!) It records the current, maximum and minimum temperatures, both outside and inside, to an accuracy of 0.5°C. It set me back all of $6.95. I've also purchased a more up-market model from Dick Smith Electronics in the form of a *TempTec* Hygrometer and In/Out Thermometer. For $50 it contains all of the features of the Coyote model, but with accuracy to 0.1°C, plus a hygrometer with minimum and maximum memory to monitor humidity. Variations are available at almost any price point.

If you are prepared to go to a little extra trouble, a few small modifications make the *TempTec* unit an even more useful device for cellar monitoring.

These are by no means essential, but can make the unit more convenient for use in the cellar. Although one of its temperature probes is connected to the unit by a long wire, both the other probe and the humidity probe are inside the casing. This is not ideal if you want to observe cellar conditions from outside.

Temptec Thermometer/Hygrometer Modifications

Relocating the two probes is not a difficult task for anyone who has used a soldering iron. It's also quite safe.

Unscrew the back panel from the unit and unscrew the circuit board at the bottom. Turn it over and note the probes soldered to the board. The temperature probe is the little round blue one; the humidity probe the rectangular white one. Desolder them from the board, being careful not to overheat the temperature probe (I use pointy nosed pliers to hold the legs of the probe and to act as a heatsink). Solder the ends of a pair of two-core cables to the points where the probes were located. Fine speaker wire is useful for this purpose. Solder the other ends of the cables to the two probes. Where the cables exit the device cut the hole slightly larger to accommodate the new wires.

Now waterproof the temperature probe. In the past I have made the mistake of using a glob of superglue for this purpose. The problem with this method is that it results in slightly incorrect readings from the probe. A small waterproof tube such as a sealed biro casing would be more reliable. Insert the probe and pop it into an empty wine bottle.

Find a used cork in good condition, and cut a small slit along its length to enable the wire to sit just inside it when the cork is inserted in the bottle. Fill the bottle with water, and cork it as best you can. I find that with enough pushing and hitting, the cork will eventually go right in (provided the bottle isn't overfilled). If it doesn't make a waterproof seal (mine usually doesn't!) then seal over the cork with superglue and/or melted candle wax. This device will monitor the air temperature, bottle temperature and humidity in the cellar.

The first time I completed this modification my friends became quite worried. With wires protruding from the wax seal on the bottle, they assumed that I had developed an interest in explosive Acme Coyote contraptions! Why one would plant an explosive in the middle of their wine cellar is beyond me. To the contrary, this device will enable you to monitor the well-being of your wines for years to come.

Cellaring locations

Armed with this new contraption, you can set out to investigate some potential cellaring locations. A good start is an inside room, one that does not have any exterior walls to heat up in the sun. A linen cupboard in such a room is even better. A little extra protection can be provided in such locations by leaving wines in their cases, or even wrapping bottles in newspaper. In any case, bottles sealed with natural cork should be cellared horizontally to ensure that the cork stays moist. Remember that in any location, it is the extremes of temperature that are most telling, so be sure to note summer maximums.

Underground cellars are an excellent option, but may prove to be a lot of trouble for little gain. Some years ago I spent a few weekends digging under our house. The project came to an abrupt halt when I discovered that even the ground undergoes an annual variation of some 10°C. My underground cellar would have required practically as much insulation and artificial cooling as an aboveground cellar.

If you find a location in your home to be satisfactory according to the conditions outlined in Chapter 2, by all means make the most of it. Unfortunately, for the majority of us, some additional strategies will be required. It is to these that we now turn our attention.

Cellaring Wine: do-it-yourself solutions

Polystyrene boxes can make an excellent first cellar

4. Where do I Start?

A beginner's cellar

One of the most revealing experiences that I have had with the changes that occur in wine as it ages was in the form of a vertical tasting of Tahbilk Marsanne. Some Australian wineries are beginning to hold back vintages of their classic wines for release as mature bottles. Tahbilk recently made available vintages of its Marsanne from the past twelve years. I assembled a group of friends and we tasted our way from 1998 back to 1988.

The contrast could not have been stronger. The 1998 was a fresh, acidic wine, very light green-yellow in colour and displaying an intense variety of fruit flavours including tropical fruits, lime and gooseberries. The 1988 was golden yellow/orange and was both incredibly intense and very smooth and integrated. The acid was soft and all of its primary fruit flavours had been replaced with rich butterscotch, honey and a touch of camphor. Both wines were quite superb, but the complete contrast of their styles made it very difficult to believe that they were the same wine. The magic of the cellar is a truly fascinating phenomenon. But it must be nurtured carefully if it is to work its spell.

As we have seen, the biggest evil to permeate a cellar and slowly destroy bottles is temperature variation. While white wines are most sensitive to this deterioration, all wines require a stable environment in order to mature to their potential. The good news is that it doesn't take expensive technological weapons to confront this problem.

Insulated storage solutions

The first foe to overcome is also the most deadly: daily temperature variation. It is rapid temperature fluctuation that most quickly deteriorates wine. The single most effective weapon against this is insulation.

While cardboard boxes and newspaper provide some insulation, there is a better alternative that is equally inexpensive. Supermarkets and greengrocers often have an oversupply of polystyrene broccoli boxes, and many are happy to give these away. At worst, they will set you back a few

Cellaring Wine: do-it-yourself solutions

dollars. These boxes come with airtight lids and are easily stacked. They are the perfect size to house 18 bottles and still allow room for layers of newspaper to provide further insulation. By storing wines close together in this way, the effect of 'safety in numbers' also promotes temperature stability, as the 'thermal mass' (temperature retention ability) of many bottles resists rapid fluctuation.

I monitored the temperature in such boxes in a cool location in my home over a period of six months. The daily temperature variation of the air in the boxes never exceeded 1°C, while the weekly variation was always less than 2 °C. The bottle temperature variation was slightly less than this again. This is a significant improvement over the 10°C range in the daily room temperature in the same room. However, this system does little to combat seasonal temperature variation, with the boxes as low as 15°C in mid-winter and as high as 28.5°C at the height of summer. Nonetheless, the elimination of rapid temperature variation is an excellent first step.

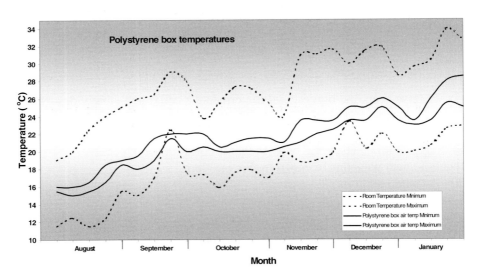

But is this good enough? It would be reasonable to assume that the size of one's cellar has a bearing on the amount of time that wines will be left to mature. While a cellar of several hundreds of bottles may allow for years of cellaring, it is unrealistic to expect a collection of 30 or 40 bottles to sit for many years, despite the best of intentions! This fact also makes the task of planning storage conditions more straightforward. One would naturally go to more trouble for a large collection that needs to survive for many years. With this in mind, simple inexpensive solutions such as polystyrene boxes may be quite adequate for a small wine cellar.

A second reason for which such boxes are best suited to smaller collections is that of accessibility. While the boxes can be stacked, this makes access to bottles in the bottom box difficult. In addition, unless bottles are packed such that one box contains only multiples of a single wine, accessing a particular bottle can necessitate disturbing a number of others. For larger collections, this can be quite impractical, and alternatives should be considered.

My father-in-law's cellar is located under a stairwell in the centre of his house. The area was conveniently walled-off when the house was built, with large cupboard doors installed to allow access. While the space was perfect, the temperature was not. Not wanting to go to too much expense, he opted for a simple insulating system. I donated some sheets of five-centimetre thick polystyrene that were left over from some of my own cellar projects. After lining the walls, doors and the underside of the stairs above, the temperature stability of the space was improved considerably.

Those of us who have an area that is as convenient as this are fortunate indeed. For the rest of us, there is another alternative that is just as effective and not much more expensive.

Cellaring Wine: do-it-yourself solutions

An old fridge is a simple but effective cellar for up to about 120 bottles

5. Raid the Fridge

A climate-controlled cellar for $120

It was around the same time as my wine collection doubled in size that I first became interested in establishing ideal storage conditions. My wife Rachael and I had just returned from a trip to South Australia. Having spent the first week of our holiday visiting relatives, we spent the second touring the Barossa Valley. An intensive schedule of visiting historic wineries, talking to winemakers and sampling from barrels and bottles quickly led to a new appreciation for this fascinating product. That trip opened up my palate to a quality of wine that I had never before experienced.

Within a month, my cellar had expanded from three or four dozen bottles to double that number. When previously I had been reluctant to spend more than $8 on a bottle, I now saw the quantum leap in quality that was possible by spending $15. I was then faced with the question of how to store this growing collection. At this time I was given a copy of James Halliday's book *Collecting Wine: You and Your Cellar* (Harper Collins, 1998). This book further aroused my interest, particularly in the amazing transformations that can occur in wine as it ages. It also taught me about the importance of ideal cellaring conditions. Thus began what has since become a long-term pursuit to achieve these conditions in an average home on a small budget. The first idea came from a winemaker during that visit to the Barossa Valley.

The wine fridge

The weekly 'For Sale' column of any newspaper is lined with devices that make excellent homes for a small wine collection. Not only are they inexpensive and convenient, but they are also surprisingly effective. It was Robert Schrapel of Bethany Wines who proposed the simplest and most economical climate-controlled cellar: the humble refrigerator.

Within a couple of months of returning from the Barossa, I acquired my first wine cellar: a 350L Kelvinator 'fridge only', which I picked up second-hand for $40. Around $100 would be a reasonable price for which to aim, but there are occasional bargains such as this one. It ran surprisingly well, although this was of little consequence at the time as I only planned to use it as a big insulated cupboard. I arranged the shelves to each hold a few rows of bottles, with a total capacity of about 120 bottles. A slight odour was eliminated by placing an open container of bicarbonate of soda inside the unit. Monitoring the air temperature inside the fridge over a year revealed a weekly variation of 1°C to 2°C and a seasonal variation of 10°C. These results were similar to those of my polystyrene broccoli boxes.

There were a few things that I looked for when searching for an old fridge for wine storage. First, the old metal grille shelves could handle the weight of a number of rows of bottles much better than the modern flimsy plastic shelves. Secondly, I avoided frost-free units. If I ever needed to run the cooling system, such a unit would dehumidify the air and potentially dry out corks. A 'fridge only' was also more convenient than the more common fridge/freezer combination. Storage capacity was slightly larger, and it avoided the potential problem of a 'super-chilled' freezer section. A friend with such a unit experiences problems with condensed moisture in the freezer every time the refrigerator completes its regular cycle. In addition to these design characteristics, the condition of the unit is naturally also important. The state of the door seals is particularly significant, as these have a large bearing on the effectiveness of the insulation. Ideally, the seals should be soft and should make a tight seal around the entire door. If this is not the case, they can be replaced, but this can become expensive.

This first refrigerator proved to be quite an effective unit for short-term wine storage. It offered an advantage of accessibility that my broccoli boxes did not. By numbering shelves and recording bottle locations in my cellar record book, I could locate and remove a bottle quickly and with disruption to no more than a few other bottles. I was quite pleased with the reduction in weekly temperature variation that the fridge provided. However, the annual temperature range was still something of a concern. During a particularly hot summer week, the temperature in my fridge hit 25°C. A friend with a similar unit in his garage reported an astonishing 32°C. Something had to be done.

Here began my pursuit of a fully climate-controlled cellar. Up until now the cellars that we have considered have functioned passively, relying purely on insulation to protect our precious bottles from the harmful effects of temperature variation. But with the exception of some very cool and stable locations in southern Australia, any long-term cellar will require active temperature control. This is, of course, available via expensive commercial solutions, but it is by no means out of reach of the small collector and his or her small budget.

The climate-controlled wine fridge

A climate-controlled cellar can be as simple as a domestic refrigerator that is allowed to run. The second refrigerator that I purchased for wine storage was a 350L Whirlpool unit. It was practically a giveaway at $20, because it did not get cool enough for the freezer to operate. This suited my needs perfectly. On testing it I discovered that the thermostat was faulty and was operating at 16°C rather than the standard 4°C. This was quite a stroke of luck! More often, however, we need to go to a little more trouble in order to enable a refrigerator to operate at higher temperatures.

Thermostats

Standard refrigerator thermostats are inadequate for cellaring wine on two counts. The first is simply that they are rarely able to be adjusted

Caution!

Modification of any electrical appliance requires verification by a certified electrician. All electrical wiring work referred to in this book should only be attempted by qualified personnel.

above about 8–10°C. The second problem is less obvious but more important. The 'temperature differential' is too large. The temperature differential of a thermostat is the difference between the temperature at which it turns on and the temperature at which it turns off. For instance, a thermostat that turns on when the temperature reaches 6°C and off again at 2°C would have a 4°C differential. Such a differential is typical for many refrigeration thermostats, but it introduces a problem in our wine cellar. If the air temperature varies by 4°C every time the cooling system comes on, the bottle temperature will vary frequently, and we undo the main purpose of cooling altogether.

A thermostat with a small differential is required. I sourced a 'Capillary thermostat' from a firm called RS Components (stock number 250-6061). It cost about $40. Refer to their website at www.rs-components.com.au for full details. It is variable between -30°C and +35°C and has a differential of 1.5°C, small enough for the air cycle not to vary the bottle temperature.

Cellaring Wine: do-it-yourself solutions

A plastic 'jiffy' box makes a good home for a replacement thermostat

The advantage of the capillary system is that it enables the thermostat control to be placed outside of the cellar environment, although this is not always important. An electrician should be able to complete the thermostat exchange at minimal cost, particularly if you are able to mount the new thermostat yourself and just leave the wiring to him or her. I have found that a plastic 'jiffy' box available from electronics suppliers such as Dick Smith Electronics is a good way to mount the unit.

Placement of the thermostat probe about two-thirds of the way up the cabinet seems to be ideal. There is something of a compromise involved here, and some experimentation may be necessary. If the thermostat is directly in the air flow close to the cooling unit, it may cause the cycle to be very rapid, with the unit turning on and off too regularly. On the other hand, if the thermostat is too far out of the air flow, a slow cycle will cause the bottle temperature to rise and fall slightly during each cycle.

A good alternative to the capillary thermostat is a digital unit. These are available from commercial refrigeration suppliers and offer a number of advantages over the standard analogue devices. First, the temperature is entered exactly, rather than simply rotating a dial and hoping that it is right. Secondly, and more significantly, these units also enable the differential to be adjusted. This can eliminate some of the experimentation with placement that is necessary with other thermostats. These devices also provide exact temperature readouts and detailed programming and control facilities. Unfortunately, such luxuries come at a price — around $160. This was more than I could justify.

Air flow

The next step in setting up your refrigerator is to ensure that the air flow is adequate. While some fridges have a built-in fan to cater for this, others may require more attention. A small $15 desk fan from Big W is an economical solution. This can be wired to operate when the thermostat turns on. Placing the fan near the cooling unit such that it creates an air flow throughout the cabinet helps to ensure even dissipation of the cool air. Even with this in place, I have found that my unit maintains a constant bottle temperature of 12°C at the top near the cooling unit, 16°C halfway down and 19 °C at the bottom. This performance is similar to that of equivalent commercial wine-storage units. Given that the temperatures are stable, such variation within the cabinet does not concern me too much for medium-term cellaring.

A small fan can improve distribution of cool air throughout the cellar

Some simpler options

Adding a new thermostat to a refrigerator could prove to be more trouble and expense than you are prepared to accept. There is a simpler solution that, while less effective, can help to reduce seasonal variation. During the warmer months of the year, I connected my refrigerator to a timer unit that was able to turn it on and off several times a day. Such units are commonly available for $10-$15, and can be plugged in directly without requiring any rewiring. With the fridge turning on for half-hour bursts during the warmest parts of the day, I was able to 'chop off' the summer maximum temperatures by at least a few degrees. While this was still not ideal for long-term cellaring, it did produce a cellar suitable for medium-term propositions. Four of our seven conditions for ideal cellaring were satisfied: a reasonably stable temperature, a low temperature, darkness and low ventilation. Chapter 8 details some strategies for controlling humidity. When it comes to establishing a more stable environment for serious cellaring, slightly more advanced options need to be considered.

Cellaring Wine: do-it-yourself solutions

The author and a drinks fridge with a difference

6. When Size Does Matter

A cellar for 250 bottles

The question: 'How big?' is one that every wine collector ends up facing at some stage. The answer is the product of two questions: 'How much do you drink?' and 'How long do you intend to cellar it?' When I include bottles that we open at home, those we take to dinners, bottles for tasting events, gifts, and the odd one that will end up at auction, my answer to the first question is about 150 bottles per year. Cellaring time will, of course, vary for different bottles, some lasting for only weeks after purchase, with others laying dormant for a decade or more. On average, about five and a half years seems right for my collection. My annual consumption of 150 bottles multiplied by 5.5 years means that I need to allow for an ongoing capacity of some 825 bottles. Total capacity dictates the size of the storage facility.

Number of bottles in the cellar	=	Number of bottles consumed per year	X	Average number of years of cellaring per bottle

The big wine fridge

When my cellar outgrew a standard refrigerator, I began considering commercial refrigeration units. I figured that a drinks fridge, such as the ones used by service stations and convenience stores, could be modified to hold between 200 and 400 bottles. After pricing a suitable unit at between $900 and $1000 at local second-hand commercial appliance outlets, I was pleased to find one privately for $450. It had two glass doors and four shelves, with the compressor mounted at the bottom.

Thermostats

My first job was to get the temperature right. After cleaning up the unit, I was quite excited to discover that the thermostat not only had variable temperature control but also a variable differential. In the hope that I could avoid replacing the thermostat, I experimented with levels for a few days. Alas, while it would happily run at 15°C, the differential was far too high at 4–5°C.

Cellaring Wine: do-it-yourself solutions

Bottles in the cellar, with the thermostat visible on the bottom right. The water and towel system is used to maintain humidity levels (see Chapter 8).

A new thermostat was required, so I purchased another 250-6061 capillary unit from RS Components (see page 27). Before I installed it, I checked the electrical current handling capacity of the thermostat contacts and discovered that this was lower than the current draw of the refrigerator. (If in doubt, an electrician could make this decision for you.) A $20 AC relay from RS Components solved the problem. The thermostat turned the relay on and off which in turn controlled the refrigerator. I mounted the thermostat control inside the cabinet rather than outside. I had found from previous experimentation with these units that while they are supposed to rely only on the temperature of the capillary probe itself, the temperature of the control unit seemed to affect its performance ever so slightly. I housed the thermostat in a plastic jiffy box at the bottom of the inside of the cabinet and ran the wiring through the base to the wiring box underneath. An electrician could complete the job from there.

Racking system

With a stable and low temperature under control my next priority was in establishing a racking system to hold the bottles. While the existing wire shelves were rigid enough to support dozens of bottles, I opted to remove them in favour of a system that would enable a bottle to be removed without disturbing numerous others. After investigating a number of racking options, I settled on one that was simple, effective and relatively inexpensive. ARC Smorgon sells a *Weldmesh* product consisting of 4mm diameter wires welded into a grid of 10cm square holes. Although it is intended for concrete reinforcement, the size of the holes in this product is ideal for racking standard 750mL bottles. One 3.0m x 2.4m sheet was ample for this project, and cost $70. I obtained the galvanised version in

When Size Does Matter

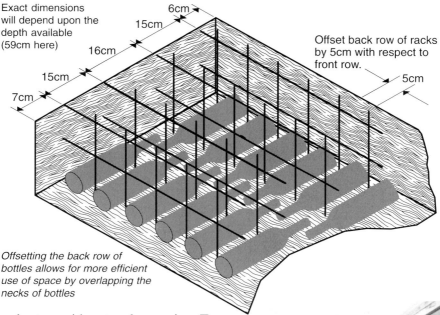

Offsetting the back row of bottles allows for more efficient use of space by overlapping the necks of bottles

order to avoid rust and corrosion. Two parallel sheets suspended vertically about 15–20cm apart provided a very sturdy and inexpensive racking system and allowed for good air flow around the bottles. I have also seen *Weldmesh* with 20cm spaces used effectively, with the advantage of allowing for five standard bottles per space.

With an interior depth of 59cm in the cabinet and an average bottle height of about 30cm, I needed to be creative in order to make optimal use of the space. After much thought and experimentation, I settled on a system by which the bottles are stored two bottles deep. The back row is accessed by removing a bottle from the front row. This has not proven to be too inconvenient, since most bottles in the

A Weldmesh *racking system is inexpensive but effective*

33

Cellaring Wine: do-it-yourself solutions

Space above the racks allows for storage of larger format bottles. Timber edging supports the racks.

back are the same wine as the bottles immediately in front of them anyway. In order to maximise space, I offset the back row of bottles by exactly half a bottle width in relation to the front row (see diagram on previous page). This meant that when the back-row bottles were placed in neck-forward and the front row neck-back, the tops of the bottles lay alternately alongside each other, thus reducing the required depth of the cabinet. To support the bottles, I cut the *Weldmesh* into four sheets using bolt cutters. The back two sheets were mounted by offsetting them by 5cm horizontally from the front two sheets. This enabled enough overlap for the bottles to fit comfortably within the 59cm depth. Another method that has been suggested is to use three sheets of *Weldmesh*, with the bottles placed in a similar fashion as in my system, but sharing the middle rack to support their necks. Unusually shaped bottles could pose a problem here.

While the *Weldmesh* is ideal for standard bottles, the holes are not quite big enough for some sparkling wine bottles and most larger format bottles such as magnums. To allow for these I left a 23cm gap between the top of the racking and the top of the fridge. This provided room to stack a couple of rows of these bottles. This allowance proved to be essential anyway, since the height of the doors through which I installed the racks was smaller than the interior height of the cabinet.

In order to attach the racks, I decided to construct timber frames to run around the outside of each sheet of *Weldmesh*. 19x42mm pine proved to be the most economical option. I cut the *Weldmesh* such that about 19mm of wire protruded from each side, which then slotted into holes that I drilled in the timber frames. By screwing the frames together at the top and bottom around the *Weldmesh* and then screwing them into the interior of the cabinet, I was able to produce a very stable rack. I positioned each pair of sheets about 15cm apart, with a gap of 16cm between the two pairs. This method of attaching the racks is probably a little more time-intensive than is really necessary, but it does produce quite a professional-looking result. A simpler solution may be just to screw the *Weldmesh* directly into the cabinet by alternating flat-head screws on either side of the sheets. If this option were chosen, I would still suggest running a timber support along the top and bottom of each of the sheets. This not only keeps them straight, avoiding the dangerous tendency of the racks to bulge outwards, but it also provides more even distribution of the weight at the bottom, and support for magnums at the top. Keep in mind that 250 bottles have a mass of more than one third of a tonne. A final option would be to weld the sheets into place — an excellent possibility if you have the equipment to do so.

Darkness

Eliminating the light that entered the cabinet was my next challenge. This came from two sources: the fluorescent light inside the unit and the clear-glass doors. Most commercial drinks fridges are set up with a light that runs continually. Mine was no exception, so I rewired the fluorescent tube so that it was controlled via a switch on the front of the unit. I covered it in two layers of ultraviolet tinting film to produce more gentle light. After considering fully blacking out the glass on the doors, I decided that the cabinet would look better if I simply darkened it instead. Since ultraviolet light is the most damaging to wines, I chose a dark ultraviolet tinting film. It cost about $30 from a local car accessories outlet and was surprisingly easy to apply without bubbling. The result enabled me to just see the bottles on the inside. With the flourescent light on, it gave the bottles an eerie glow which looked quite cool! It also helped in locating them without opening the door for long periods, and potentially disrupting the temperature balance inside.

Tinted glass doors can protect bottles from harmful ultraviolet light

Indexing system

To further aid in keeping track of bottles, an indexing system is vital for a collection of this size. My cabinet contains ten rows and fifteen columns, which provides for a total capacity of about 250 bottles (accounting for some loss of space due to interior fixtures). I chose to label the locations in a similar fashion to a spreadsheet, with the rows labelled numerically and the columns alphabetically. Stick-on vinyl letters and numbers from a stationery supplier proved to be ideal for labelling each row and column. Each location could then be referenced with, for instance, F13f ('f' denoting 'front', although the front/back identifier is usually unnecessary). These coded identifiers are recorded next to each bottle in my cellar inventory book. This document also helps in progressively keeping track of the best time to drink each bottle.

Tyson and Rachael's Wine Cellar Inventory

Winery	Vintage	Variety	From	For	On	No	Tasting Notes	Date	Optimal Drinking	Location
Bethany	1996	GR4 Shiraz	Cellar Door	$60	8/01	1	12/01 Big raspberry & cherry fruit, vanillin oak; a smooth mouthfeel and long finish. Great wine that needs a few more years to show its best.		2004-2006?	B6
						1				

Vibration

The next evil to eliminate in my cellar cabinet was vibration. With a reasonably large compressor underneath, a lot of vibration was transferred throughout the cabinet. By comparison, the circulation fans both inside and outside of the unit produced negligible disruption. My priority in eliminating vibration was therefore to isolate the compressor. This could be achieved by supporting its weight without relying on the frame of the cabinet. I unscrewed the compressor unit from its base and cut holes with an electric jigsaw in the platform on which it was mounted. By making these holes slightly larger than building bricks, I could support the compressor on two bricks. It sits slightly higher than its original position, but with the bricks removed, it can be screwed back into place for

When Size Does Matter

transportation. In its new position its full weight is supported by the ground via the bricks, and consequently the vibration transferred to the wines is imperceptible.

The compressor under the fridge, mounted on bricks to reduce the transfer of vibration

Air circulation

With the unit complete, I spent a number of weeks tweaking its performance. In particular, the location of the thermostat and the level of air flow needed to be optimised. It was also necessary to increase the relative humidity (see full details in Chapter 8).

On experimenting with different thermostat locations, I found that the best position was a little over half-way up at the back. In this location it was right in the air flow produced by the fan in the cooling unit. It would turn on frequently enough to maintain a variation of only 0.2°C in the bottle temperature, but not so frequently that the unit was forever turning on and off.

It seemed that the unit was functioning perfectly, but on measuring the bottle temperature at the top and bottom of the cabinet, I was disappointed to find a 5°C difference. I wanted all of my bottles to be close to 15°C, not just somewhere between 13°C and 18°C. With the cooling unit at the bottom, the air was simply not circulating enough to adequately cool the top of the cabinet. The solution was to install a fan to increase the air flow.

The existing fan that pulled air through the cooling unit at the bottom was quite large and produced a stiff air flow. I was worried that it was producing too much breeze, so I had already suppressed it by placing a grille in front of it and rewiring it so that it only operated when the thermostat was on. Adding a speed control proved to be unsuccessful, as the motor driving the fan was a 'synchronous' motor (that is, it relied on a 50Hz AC supply to operate at 50 revolutions per second). It wasn't in a position to throw air right to the top of the cabinet, anyway. In order to achieve this, I needed a smaller fan mounted higher up that could operate when the cooling system did not.

I purchased an 8cm rotary fan from Dick Smith Electronics for about $37. It could be wired to operate from 240VAC, and it utilised ball bearings to ensure a long life and ultra-smooth operation. My thermostat had contacts that provided power when the thermostat was off, so it was a simple task to wire it to operate as soon as the cooling unit cut out. I mounted it half way up the cabinet, firing upwards. It did help in establishing a more uniform temperature, but it was still not as consistent as I required. Dick Smith Electronics allowed me to exchange it for a 12cm fan of the same type. This had a significantly larger air flow and produced an excellent result. I was not concerned about the increased ventilation, as there was no abrupt temperature variation associated with this moving air. A better alternative to purchasing a rotary fan is to source an 80mm fan from the power supply of an old computer. These can operate from a 12V DC power source and are readily obtained at no cost from discarded computers.

Performance

In its completed state, this cabinet represents nigh-on perfect cellaring conditions. In any given week, the bottle temperature varies by around 0.2°C and rarely ever more than 1°C. The seasonal variation is less than 2°C. Humidity is adequate (see Chapter 8) and ultraviolet light is eliminated. Vibration is negligible, and ventilation is maintained at reasonable levels. Under these conditions, wines will mature slowly and gracefully for their maximum expected lifetime. The only limitation of this cellar is its capacity.

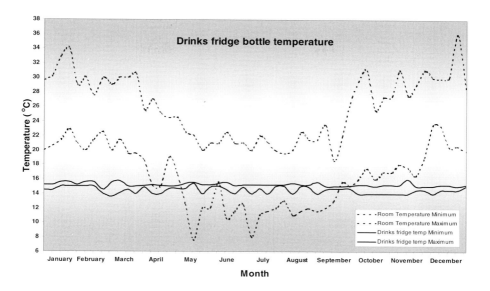

Budget

Approximate materials costs, in Australian dollars:

Second-hand drinks fridge	$450
Weldmesh for racking	70
Timber framing	20
Thermostat	40
UV tinting foil	30
Relay and electrical components	20
Hardware and fittings	20
Rotary fan	40
Digital thermometer	50
Other	10
Total	**$750**

Total cost per bottle (250 bottles): $3
Annual running cost: ~$30/year
Approximate construction time: two weekends

Cellaring Wine: do-it-yourself solutions

For those who are a little more daring, a custom-built cabinet can form the ultimate storage facility

7. Visions of Grandeur

A custom cellar cabinet

Some wines simply demand the utmost in storage conditions. The longer that a wine ages, the more the effects of an imperfect cellar take their toll. This is particularly an issue for those wines that are designed to be cellared long-term, for ten years or more. Wynns John Riddoch Coonawarra Cabernet is a classic example of such a wine.

Every now and then, one of the members of my wine-tasting group will delve into his cellar to present a special vertical tasting. Our John Riddoch evening was the very first of these. The flight spanned 1988 to 1996, and showed the younger wines to be quite unapproachable. Even at four and six years old respectively, the 1996 and 1994 were huge wines with very high levels of tannin and acid that had not yet allowed the fruit to show through. By contrast, the 1990 and 1991, while equally huge, showed layers of sweet plum fruit, liquorice, tobacco and cigar box, with well balanced tannin and acidity.

While John Riddoch is not a wine that I can normally afford due to its super-premium price tag, it does provide a good example of the many Australian wines that simply demand to be cellared. And many of them retail for a fraction of the cost of John Riddoch. It was wines such as these that inspired me to embark on my most ambitious cellar project.

My friends said it could not be done, and others said I was crazy. Perhaps there is some truth in the latter, but after months of research and construction, I now enjoy a fully climate-controlled cellar cabinet that holds 500 bottles at a total cost of only $2 per bottle. Despite some amateur experience in building and restoring furniture, this proved to be the biggest and most daring construction project that I have attempted. I would recommend such a project to those who share my daring handyman bent. But if I were to do it again, I would tend toward the simpler task of modifying a commercial drinks fridge (see Chapter 6). If this is you, you may wish to go straight to Chapter 8 at this point.

Cooling system

It took some six months to plan and design this unit. The biggest question was that of how to cool it. After some investigation, I discovered that a commercial air-conditioner would not be suitable. Even the smallest unit would be far too powerful for a cabinet with a volume of only a couple of cubic metres. The efficiency of such a combination would leave a lot to be desired, and it would also disrupt the humidity balance too much to be controllable. It appeared that the best option would be to somehow fit a cooling element (evaporator) inside, in a similar fashion to a standard refrigerator. With this in mind, I looked into a dedicated commercial refrigeration unit, but this proved to be unreasonably expensive. Then I had a strange idea. My old domestic wine fridge would soon become redundant, so why not use its cooling system in the new cabinet?

Any comments of 'It can't be done!' from sceptical friends only spurred me on to ensure that it *could* be done. A friendly retired engineer in Sydney confirmed this by completing a full heat-transfer analysis that predicted an annual running cost of only $26. After cutting the outer skin of my fridge like a sardine tin and pulling out all the pipes and electricals, I ended up with a fully operational stand-alone refrigeration system. Unfortunately, a couple of the pipes were corroded and a week later one sprang a leak. After a $100 re-gas and a few new parts, it was better than ever.

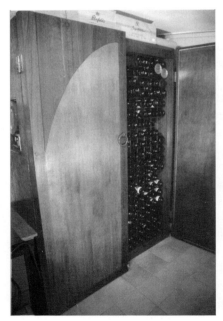

The cabinet consists of a timber frame, polystyrene insulation, Weldmesh *racks, and is finished with timber panels*

Insulation

I built the cabinet from scratch, bolting pine stud together for the frame and panelling it with sheets of three-ply timber. The doors were constructed in a similar fashion, with Jarrah edging for a visual feature.

Visions of Grandeur

The evaporator was installed at the top, running along most of the length of the cabinet. I attached the condenser (heat dissipation grille) to the outside surface, in a similar fashion to a standard refrigerator.

The key to both efficiency and stable temperature lies in effective insulation. After doing some research, I discovered that one of the cheapest insulation materials would also prove to be the most effective: polystyrene foam. While refrigerators and commercial wine cooling cabinets use about 4–5cm of insulation, I decided to double the effectiveness and use 10cm thick polystyrene. The thicker the better. In addition, the less dense grades of polystyrene offer the most effective insulation and, conveniently, are also the cheapest. A trip to a local *Koolfoam* polystyrene factory yielded (very large) off-cuts at half price, which made the cost around $100. That represented a *lot* of polystyrene, more than enough for this project.

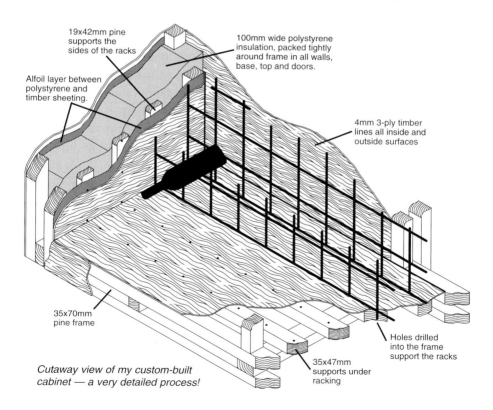

Cutaway view of my custom-built cabinet — a very detailed process!

Cellaring Wine: do-it-yourself solutions

In an attempt to reduce transfer of both radiant heat and moisture through the walls, I wanted to line both the inside and outside surfaces of the polystyrene with reflective "thermofoil". This proved to be too expensive, however, so I instead purchased about ten rolls of the cheapest aluminium foil that I could find at my local Coles supermarket. This was just as effective as thermofoil, and less than a quarter of the price. The outside and inside walls, roof, floor and doors of the cabinet consist of 4mm thick 3-ply timber, with the alfoil and polystyrene sandwiched in between. The insulating performance of this system has proved to be excellent, keeping the cabinet at a very stable, low temperature.

With such effective insulation in place, my next design challenge was to ensure an airtight seal around the (very large) doors. A friendly refrigeration-seals tradesman offered to custom-assemble some magnetic seals for me at a discounted rate of about $35 each. He arranged them in a chocolate-brown colour to match the cabinet. I chose magnetic seals to enable the doors to seal effectively without heavy catches to hold them closed. The only problem was that my cabinet was made of timber, so I needed to fit metallic strips around the door seals to ensure that they 'stuck'. But nothing ever turns out perfectly straight or square, so the doors didn't line up exactly. A few hours of wedging narrow spacers behind the seals in the right places ensured that the doors now seal as well as an average refrigerator.

Air circulation

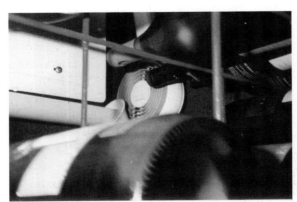

A small fan firing along the evaporator (cooling unit) can improve distribution of the cool air. Also visible here is the moisture drain under the evaporator.

To help circulate the air from the cooling unit, I found a small 'diffuse hair dryer' for five dollars at a second-hand shop (I had not yet discovered the rotary fans available from old computers.) After removing the heating element, I found that it would run off an 18V DC

Visions of Grandeur

supply quite well. A small transformer was adequate to power it. The 13cm fan from the hairdryer fires along the length of the evaporator, ensuring that the air moves over it quickly, and circulates evenly throughout the cabinet.

Vibration

I mounted the compressor in the back corner of the cabinet, but I wanted to ensure that the vibrations that it produced would not be transferred throughout the unit. I also wanted to insulate it from the inside of the cabinet to ensure that

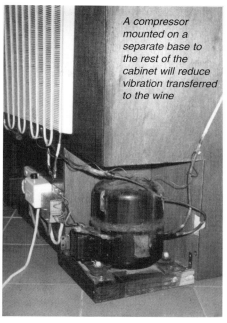

A compressor mounted on a separate base to the rest of the cabinet will reduce vibration transferred to the wine

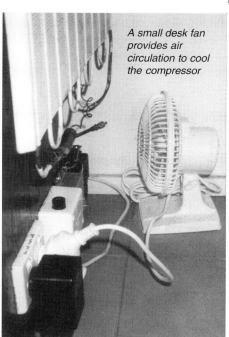

A small desk fan provides air circulation to cool the compressor

no heat would be transferred. To achieve these goals, I built a base for the compressor that was not attached to the rest of the cabinet, except during transportation, at which time it could be bolted into place. By moving it out by a few millimetres during operation, the only means for transfer of vibration was through the pipes, and this turned out to be negligible. In an attempt to both increase the efficiency of the cooling system and to reduce the strain on the compressor, I positioned a small desk fan to cool the compressor while it was running. This proved to be quite important during the warm summer months.

Racking system

In planning the layout of my cellar, I wanted to store around 400 to 500 bottles in a manner that made them easily accessible but that consumed as little floor space as possible. My constraints on the width and depth of the cabinet lay in the requirement to get it through a standard doorway. The height was restricted by the height of the room. In order to maximise the capacity within these restrictions, I opted for a *Weldmesh* racking system similar to that used in my commercial drinks fridge (see Chapter 6). The depth of the cabinet was the biggest problem, but by arranging the bottles two deep with their necks overlapping I ensured that it would still fit through a doorway.

In cutting the racks to shape, I allowed the wire rods at the ends to protrude by a couple of centimetres, and I drilled holes in the timber frame and inside panels to allow the racks to lock into place on both sides, top and bottom. This made construction difficult (I had to build the unit from the inside out), but it made for very stable and neat support of the racks. I decided to paint the racks a burgundy colour, although I wouldn't have bothered if I'd known how many days this task would eventually take! With 20 rows and 14 columns, I was able to achieve a total capacity of some 450 standard bottles, plus special spaces for magnums.

While the racking system provided an ideal width for standard bottles (of about 9.5cm), most magnums would not fit into this space. In order to provide for these larger bottles, I used bolt cutters to open out spaces equivalent to four standard positions at the top of the cabinet (see picture opposite). These each hold two to four magnums (or five standard bottles), allowing for the storage of up to about 40 magnums.

Indexing system

In order to avoid losing bottles in the maze of racks, I've added an indexing system to my cellar record book. This works in the same way as the record book for my commercial drinks cabinet (see page 36). In this case I opted for a more distinctive labelling system. I burned the labels into the timber along both sides, top and bottom, using a magnifying glass in the sun. This gives a deep, wide and neat burn which is much more effective than a soldering iron can produce. It looks great and makes for an interesting talking point. This indexing system enables me to open the cellar door, remove a particular bottle, and then close the door again within about five or six seconds. This is particularly useful on hot days, to ensure that the temperature in the cellar remains stable.

I have organised the bottles according to variety in columns: four columns for Shiraz, four for Cabernet, four for other reds and one for sundry wines including sparkling reds. This system gives me an instant visual check on where my cellar is lacking and where it is full at any time, making re-stocking decisions simpler. At least,

Bottles are organised into columns according to variety, with columns labeled alphabetically and rows numerically

that was the theory until my cellar became perpetually full! As my collection has expanded, I have dedicated my domestic refrigerator to quaffers, this custom cabinet to reds and the commercial drinks fridge to whites. The whites are organised in a similar fashion to the reds, with three columns each for Riesling and Semillon, two for Chardonnay and two for other whites including sparklings.

Cellar layout is very much a personal decision, and there are many formats to consider. Wines can be grouped according to country, region, variety, age, colour, weight, longevity, price and even bottle size. I chose variety because this is the basis on which I most often select a wine.

Cellaring Wine: do-it-yourself solutions

Control system

Control of the various systems in my custom cabinet is achieved via a control panel on the side of the unit. The most important control mechanism is the thermostat. I opted for another 250-6061 capillary thermostat (see page 27) and set it at 15°C. I originally intended to mount the thermostat probe in a bottle full of water (to simulate a wine bottle) but the temperature differential on the thermostat meant that this set-up would produce a wide swing in the bottle temperature during each cycle. With the probe mounted in the air about two-thirds of the way up the cabinet, the bottles typically only deviate by 0.1°C each cycle. The thermostat turns on the master power to the refrigeration mechanism, the 18V DC circuit and the small external fan to cool the compressor. The DC circuit operates the internal ventilation fan, humidity control system (see Chapter 8) and a clock.

A custom-built control panel allows all cellar processes to be continually controlled and monitored

I wanted to put in a simple and inexpensive system to monitor the time for which the unit runs each week. I decided that the easiest way to do this was to include an analogue wall clock that turned on and off with the system. After giving up hope of finding a (cheap) 240V clock, I paid $10 for a battery operated one and replaced the battery with a series of resistors to enable it to run off the 18V DC system. This process proved a little tricky, but it is now fulfilling its purpose, keeping a cumulative log of running time.

The control panel also includes three switches to manually turn on and off the thermostat, the AC circuit (refrigeration system) and the DC circuit, as well as a fan control. Being unsure of the ideal speed at which the fan should run, I fitted a control to enable the speed to be adjusted. Although it has High, Medium, Low and Off positions, I have not found it necessary to turn it down from High. Its gentle breeze successfully maintains a uniform temperature between the top and bottom of the cabinet. The fan runs off the 18V transformer, which turns on only when the thermostat turns on.

In order to keep a close eye on the exact status of the interior of the cabinet, I installed a Dick Smith *TempTec* digital thermometer/hygrometer. As with my commercial drinks fridge, probes inside the cabinet accurately measure the temperature inside the bottles, the air temperature in the cabinet and the humidity in the cabinet. Maximum and minimum memory enable me to monitor the extremes.

Budget

Approximate materials costs, in Australian dollars:

Timber framing	$100
Timber panelling	100
Refrigerator mechanism (from old refrigerator)	40
Re-gassing of refrigerator	100
Thermostat	50
Polystyrene	100
Magnetic door seals	70
Weldmesh for racking	125
Paint and stain	40
Hardware and fittings	140
Electrical wiring and fittings	85
Digital thermometer	50
Other	40
Total	**$1000**

Total cost per bottle (500 bottles): $2

Annual running cost: ~$26/year

Approximate construction time: four weeks

With inside room temperatures ranging from around 20°C to 30°C during summer, the cooling system runs for about six hours per day. Over a year (accounting for cooler temperatures in winter), this equates to a total

Cellaring Wine: do-it-yourself solutions

running cost of about $26. That's just over five cents per bottle per year — a small price to pay for the privilege of enjoying fine old wines.

Performance

After completing the cellar construction and half filling it with my wine collection at the time, I slowly dropped the temperature from about 25°C down to my target of 15°C over a few weeks. Within hours of finally reaching this temperature, Brisbane experienced a heat wave, recording the hottest January days ever! While my friends' cellars soared to over 30°C, mine did an interesting thing. Rather than rising, the bottle temperature dropped (by up to half a degree) during the warmest part of the day, rising again during the coolest part of the night. Puzzled by this behaviour, I eventually figured that the thermostat must be influenced slightly by the temperature outside the cabinet (where it is mounted). A polystyrene cover to insulate the thermostat control confirmed this.

With the cover on, the air temperature in the cabinet on an average day varies from about 14°C to 15°C, with the bottles varying from 15.9°C to 16.1°C. (This calibration error was introduced through attempting to seal the thermometer probes with superglue rather than mounting them in an airtight tube (see page 18). A third thermometer has confirmed the air

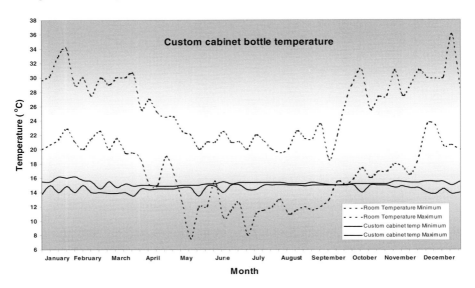

temperature readings to be correct). At the same time, humidity hovers between about 65% and 85%, dropping as low as 45% briefly when the cooling system is running. On some extreme days, the bottles may vary by up to 0.4°C, but this is rare.

When the door of the cabinet is opened, humidity naturally jumps up to 100%, as the warm moist air outside enters the cabinet and cools. This is quickly reduced again as the thermostat turns the system on after a few seconds. Bottle temperature is not affected by brief openings of the door, but if it is opened for a few minutes, the bottles may rise by up to half a degree. This system has proven to be very effective in keeping the cabinet at a stable, low temperature. Its only deficiency has been its inability to cope with the hottest weeks of summer. Under these conditions, the compressor works very hard and gets close to overheating. If I were to build such a unit again I would look for a slightly larger refrigeration unit, similar to the ones used in small commercial refrigeration machines.

Cellaring Wine: do-it-yourself solutions

*Guigal's 300-year-old cellar in the Rhone Valley, France.
The mould on the roof is a consequence of excessive humidity.*

8. Moisture Matters

Controlling humidity in the cellar

While it is common knowledge that a plant will die if allowed to dry out, few people realise that the same is true for a bottle of wine. The importance of maintaining the correct humidity in the cellar is second only to that of maintaining the right temperature. As we saw in Chapter 3, about 70% to 80% relative humidity is ideal. Not too high, for fear of mould and peeling labels, and not so low as to dry out the corks. The strategies that I have employed to control humidity have been similar in all of my cellar units. This chapter is dedicated to examining them.

While a stable temperature is more important than absolute temperature, the same is not true of humidity. It would be ideal for the humidity to be constant between 70% and 80%, but in reality a regular cycle of variation is no less ideal. Although I have not found documentation to verify this, it can be justified quite simply. Adequate humidity is primarily required for the well-being of the moisture content of the cork. Under adverse conditions, it naturally takes the cork some time to release this moisture. Hence, if the humidity varies from, say, 60% to 90% over a short cycle, then provided the average humidity is correct, the cork will be happy. The consequences of high humidity are likewise avoided over such a cycle. Mould will not develop if the moisture level fluctuates rapidly, and labels will not peel unless they are damp for some time. By a 'short cycle' I am referring to hours as opposed to days.

Strategies for reducing humidity

In designing my custom-built wine cabinet, I did some research and came to the conclusion that I was more likely to have a problem with too much humidity than too little. I soon came up with a system for reducing the humidity. The evaporator (cooling element) would freeze a considerable amount of water (condensate) around it as it ran, and this would melt as soon as it turned off. By running a drain (2 inch PVC pipe sliced in half) underneath it, I could drain the condensate through a hose and into a container outside of the cabinet (see illustration on page 44). By tilting this drain, I could control whether I wanted the water to settle and re-evaporate (to stabilise or increase humidity) or to drain off (to decrease humidity). I wanted a way to tilt this drain from an angled 'draining' position to a level 'collecting' position without opening the doors of the cabinet. I had a servo motor from an automotive central locking system lying around, and I soon discovered that it could be operated off the 18VDC system. With a suitable switch and a small spring to help it along, I had little trouble in getting it to tilt the drain enough to either catch the condensate or drain it away. In order to give an indication of the position of the drain from outside of the cabinet, I installed an LED (light) and connected it to a switch which the drain turned on when it was in a tilted position. Overkill, certainly, but such a method of draining condensate is very effective in lowering humidity in a refrigerated unit. Unfortunately, it can also be too effective!

In cellars that do not utilise such a cooling system, lowering humidity is a more challenging proposition. With commercial humidifiers ruled out due to their expense, probably the best option is to make use of some type of desiccant. Desiccants are crystalline substances that absorb moisture, and can be obtained in quantity from marine shops. Their effectiveness is limited, however, and I would sooner recommend using a cooling unit to lower the cellar temperature until the humidity drops to within the acceptable range.

Strategies for increasing humidity

Alas, theory does not always accurately predict the behaviour of the real world. It turned out that, in my wine cabinet, the drying effect of the evaporator reduced the humidity inside the cabinet to much lower levels than anticipated. My digital hygrometer revealed levels between about 40% and 60%. The tiltable drain has hence remained in the level position and I have even blocked it off slightly to enable more moisture to remain in it and evaporate. Even this did not prove to be enough to lift humidity levels adequately. I added three small open containers of water in the base of the cabinet. Still not good enough. In order to increase the surface area of evaporation, I hung a towel in a container of water. The towel acted as a wick and sped up evaporation considerably. With such a system in place, humidity now varies between about 65% and 85%, dropping to around 45% briefly when the cooling system is running. These levels are satisfactory for long-term cellaring, as most of the time the humidity hovers between about

70% and 80%. Another option that is effective in larger cellars is to use an evaporative cooling unit to increase humidity.

Controlling humidity is not just a matter of installing evaporative coolers or buckets with towel wicks. It is affected by a complex combination of factors: how long the cooling

A towel hanging in water acts as a wick to enhance evaporation and hence maintain humidity levels

system runs, how much air circulation exists, and how often the cabinet is opened. In raising the humidity levels in my commercial drinks fridge, I was faced with a more difficult task than in the case of my larger custom-built unit. In this instance, the cooling unit was much more powerful, and hence had the capability of sucking a lot more moisture out of the air. This coupled with the smaller volume of the cabinet produced a very dry result.

In overcoming this, my first target was to adjust the operating temperature. Although I was keen to cellar my white wines at 14°C, by instead opting for 15°C, the cooling system ran less and the humidity consequently rose. Naturally, the running time is determined largely by the outside ambient temperature, so the humidity drops in summer and rises in winter. This effect must be taken into consideration when designing a humidity control system, and a means for continually tweaking the system to account for seasonal variation is desirable. For me, this simply means filling or emptying evaporative containers containing towel wicks. In the case of my commercial drinks fridge, I spaced three such small containers throughout the cabinet and included a large tray at the bottom in the path of the refrigerated air flow. All four of these are necessary in summer, but in winter when the cooling system runs less, I can allow some to run dry.

Despite these measures, the humidity varied from only 52% to 75% in summer. This was still not adequate. An attempt to increase evaporation by plugging the hole that drained the condensate from the bottom of the

Cellaring Wine: do-it-yourself solutions

cabinet proved to be impractical, as the water soon formed a deep puddle that threatened to engulf some unfortunate bottles on the bottom shelf! I needed to try a different approach. I had already considered installing a small fan to provide more even air circulation. By allowing this to run whenever the cooling system was off, I could achieve two goals, by using it to also increase evaporation. I placed a container with a towel wick near it, and after upgrading to a larger fan, the humidity levels rose to between 55% and 85%, with an average around 75%.

After a little experimentation, it is possible to bring even the most stubborn systems up to satisfactory levels of humidity. Under such conditions, good corks can last practically indefinitely. Well, almost.

> 'In the case of prolonged storage,
> the corks should be changed every 20 to 30 years.'
>
> The late Jean Hugel, tenth generation winegrower, Alsace, France.

With a climate-controlled cellar, this prospect is not as ridiculous as it might sound.

The trend in cult winemaking in recent years has been toward the 'garage wines', so called because their production is small enough to occur in a garage. In Australia, cellaring trends seem to be tending in a similar direction. A 'garage cellar' may be small and makeshift, but by applying the principles outlined in this book, it can be incredibly effective. A fully functional climate-controlled cellar can fit into any garage and any budget.

The art of carefully maturing wine is a passion that can be enjoyed for many decades. It can be achieved by any 'garage' collector who is prepared to take a little initiative and be a little creative. Nurture a plant carefully and it will reward you.

I wish you many great old bottles. Happy cellaring.

Index

15ºC, 10, 17, 22, 31, 37, 48, 50, 55
accessibility, 23, 26
active temperature control, 27
air conditioner, 42
air flow, 14, 28, 29, 33, 37, 38, 44, 48, 49
Alsace, 9
aluminium foil, 44
ambient temperature, 9
Barossa Valley, 25
Bethany Wines, 25, 36
bicarbonate of soda, 26
Bin 28 Kalimna Shiraz, 4
Bordeaux, 5, 6
bottle shock, 14
broccoli boxes, 20–23, 26
budget, 15, 39, 49
Burgundy, 11
calibration, 50
capacity, 26, 31, 36, 46
capillary thermostat, 27, 28, 32, 48
cellar layout, 32, 46, 47
cellar record book, 26, 36
cellaring time, 22, 31
Champagne, 9, 10
Château de Pommard, 11, 12
Château Margaux, 6
chemical reactions, 9, 12
climate, 1, 8, 9, 22, 50
clock, 48
commercial cellars, 1, 15, 27, 29
compressor, 31, 36, 45
condenser, 43, 45
conditions, 7–14, 19, 25, 29, 38
control panel, 48
cooling, 8–10, 13–14, 19, 22, 26–29, 31, 32, 37–39, 42–45, 49–51, 54, 55
cork, 7, 8, 11, 18, 19, 26, 53, 56
cycle, 26– 28, 48

darkness, 12, 29, 35
desiccant, 54
Dick Smith, 17, 28, 38, 49
differential, 27, 28, 31, 48
digital thermometer, 16–18, 39, 48, 49
disruption, 12–14, 26, 36, 45
doors, 23, 26, 31, 34, 35, 42, 44, 46 54
drain, 44, 53, 54
drinking habits, 1
drinks fridge, 30–39
efficiency, 42, 43, 45
evaporation, 54–56
evaporator, 42–45, 53, 54
fan, 29, 36–39, 44, 45, 48, 49, 56
frames, 34, 43, 49
frost-free, 26
garage wines, 56
Gold Coast, 17
Grange, 3, 4
GR 4 Shiraz, 36
Guigal, 13, 52
Halliday, James, 25
Hugel, 9
humidity, 10–12, 17, 18, 29, 37, 42, 48, 49, 51–56
hygrometer, 17, 49, 54
indexing, 36, 46, 47
insulation, 19–23, 26, 42–44
inventory, 36
Jacob's Creek, 3
jiffy box, 28, 32
John Riddoch, 41
Kalimna Shiraz, 4
Koolfoam, 43
labels, 11, 12, 36, 46, 53
Lake's Folly, 7
leaking bottles, 7, 8, 11
light, 12, 29, 35

linen cupboard, 19
Loire Valley, 10
magnetic seals, 44, 49
magnums, 34, 35, 46
Marc Bredif, 10, 11
Marsanne, 21
mature, 1, 21, 22, 38
moisture, 26, 44, 53–56
monitor, 17, 18, 22, 48
mould, 11, 12, 53
necks, 34, 46
newspaper, 19, 21
odour, 26
Orlando, 3
oxidation, 8
panelling, 42, 49
Penfolds, 3, 4
performance, 29, 32, 37–39, 44, 50, 51
polystyrene boxes, 20–23, 26
polystyrene insulation, 21, 23, 26, 42–44, 49, 50
probe, 18, 28, 32, 48
professional wine storage, 15
racking, 32–34, 43, 46, 49
refrigerator, 7, 15, 17, 24–39, 42, 43, 44, 46, 47, 49
re-gas, 42, 49
relay, 32, 39
Rhone Valley, 13, 52
rotary fan, 38, 39
RS Components, 27, 32
safety, imprint page, 27
seals (fridge), 26, 44, 49
seasonal variation, 26, 29, 38, 55
servo motors, 54
shelves, 24, 26, 31, 32
size of cellar, 22, 26, 31, 36, 41, 46
speed (fan), 38, 48
stable temperature, 8, 9, 14, 21, 22, 29, 38, 43, 53
stairwell, 23

storage conditions, 1, 7–15, 22, 25,
switches, 48
Tahbilk, 21
Tattinger, 9
temperature, 8–10, 14, 17–19, 21–23, 26–29, 31, 32, 35, 37–39, 43, 44, 47-51, 53, 55
temperature differential, 27, 28, 31, 48
TempTec, 17, 49
thermal mass, 22
thermofoil, 44
thermometer, 16–18, 39, 49, 50
thermostat, 27–29, 31, 32, 37–39, 48–51
timer, 29
tinting film, 35, 39
towel wick, 32, 54–56
transformations, 3, 7, 21, 25
transformer, 45, 49
travel shock, 14
ultraviolet light, 12, 35, 38
underground cellars, 15, 17, 19
ventilation, 14, 28, 29, 33, 37, 38, 44, 48, 49
vibration, 12, 13, 36–38, 45
weekly variation, 9, 22, 26, 38, 39, 50
Weldmesh, 32–34, 39, 46, 49
white wines, 10, 12, 21
wick, 32, 54–56
wine rack, 1, 7, 8
wine tastings, 3, 7, 12, 21, 41
Wynns, 41